BILMA

BILMA

by

B. Wongar

Ohio State University Press : Columbus

All illustrations are taken from
*Australian Aboriginal Paintings in Western and Central Arnhem Land:
Temporal Sequences and Elements of Style in
Cadell River and Deaf Adder Creek Art*,
by E. J. Brandl.
Published in 1973 by the Australian Institute of Aboriginal Studies
in Canberra.

Copyright © 1984 by B. Wongar. All rights reserved.

Designed by Kent D. King.

Library of Congress Cataloguing in Publication Data

Wongar, B.
   Bilma.

   I. Title.
PR9619.3.W62B5   1984   821   84.5103
ISBN 0–8142–0370–1

To Miroslav Holub

Flying foxes are about again
grinding rocks
to encircle the world
with grains of sand.

Shrouded in dust
trees fall into oblivion.

What was that magic chant
to keep our heads
above the desert?

Contents

Emancipation   11
Ngir   12
Namanama   14
The Forest   15
Sugar Glider   17
Food Gatherer   23
The Tale   24
Trapped Dingo   26
Jail   27
Fertility Rites   28
The Brolgas   29
The Journey   30
New Gospel   31
The Invasion   32
Census   35
Discovery of the Boomerang   37
The Settlers   38
Pillaged Country   39
The Conquest   41

Bilma 43
Magarada 45
The Statistics 47
The Gospel (Contemporary) 50
Squatters 53
The History 54
Rodingu 56
The Cycle 57
Jabiru 59
Fertility Ritual 60
The Dust 61
The Drought 62
U_3O_8 63
Bralgu 67
An Epitaph 68

Glossary 69

BILMA

Emancipation

The first word ever to be written
came from *balanda*, "white man." Before that
the world was an empty blackboard.
Instead of books, animals and birds had a pecking order
and lived longer.

"Come out of the dark," ordered white man.
Kangaroos, cockatoos, and dingoes received little slates,
half a pencil and a sponge each.
Every soul had to write ABC.
That happened in Dreaming, time before history,
and before God had time to make water
—the beginners had to spit on the sponge to rub out the errors;

the pencils broke and the slates shattered.

"Plead quilty or not guilty," yelled *balanda*.
No one knew how to write that, so
Kangaroos, cockatoos, and dingoes were caned
in name of God
                King and
                          Justice.
When lashed over the head, the skin red with scabies,
the lice do sit still, yet
the new pecking order never was won
nor did the world learn to spell *peace*.

Ngir

Ngir, ngir . . .
—They shroud you with dust.

Ngir, ngir, ngir . . .
—Don't count dead trees,
your voice will grow hoarse.

Ngir, ngir, ngir, ngir . . .
—When you sing from the dust,
humans grow deaf.

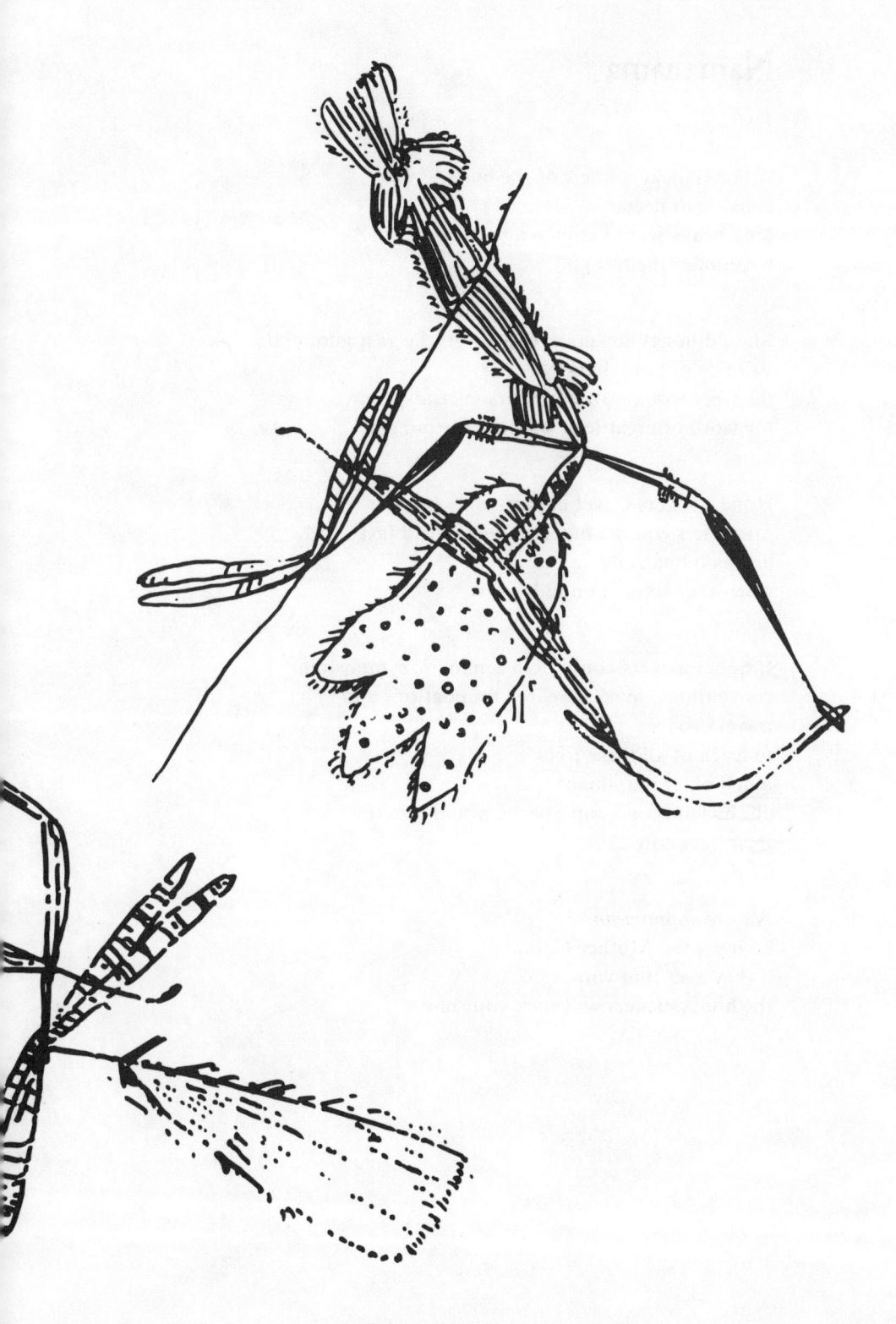

Namanama

If honeysuckers knew of the bush
laden with nectar
long beaks would stretch a half-world across
to plunder the trees.

Should honeysuckers ever learn of the vast gum plain
swamps of paperbarks
the trees would grow feathers instead of leaves
for word of great loot would get around.

Honeysuckers travel in pairs
raise their young on nectar and spread fast
just as humans do
when they sense a good harvest.

If honeysuckers could hold seminars, symposiums
conventions, make research foundations and
travel tax-free
to learn of all these trees
much older than man
all the gums and paperbarks would lose their leaves
their bark too.

Ah my *namanama*
ah my good Mother Country
if they ever find you
the honeysuckers will suck your blood.

The Forest

When pillaged the country cries
—a bee caught in a spider's web—
no soul likes to be eaten silently.

Down on Wall Street, La Bourse, and the Royal Stock Exchange
you hear wailing of rain forest,
for the trees speak all lingos;
they, too, don't like to be eaten silently.
You can hear them in much smaller places
Zurich or Lausanne
when you come down to open your vault at Trust International.

Trees have a peculiar way of creeping up to you;
they often hang around cashier's counters
rattling their leaves.
No need to alarm the security, though
—those are only the spirits of the dead forest.

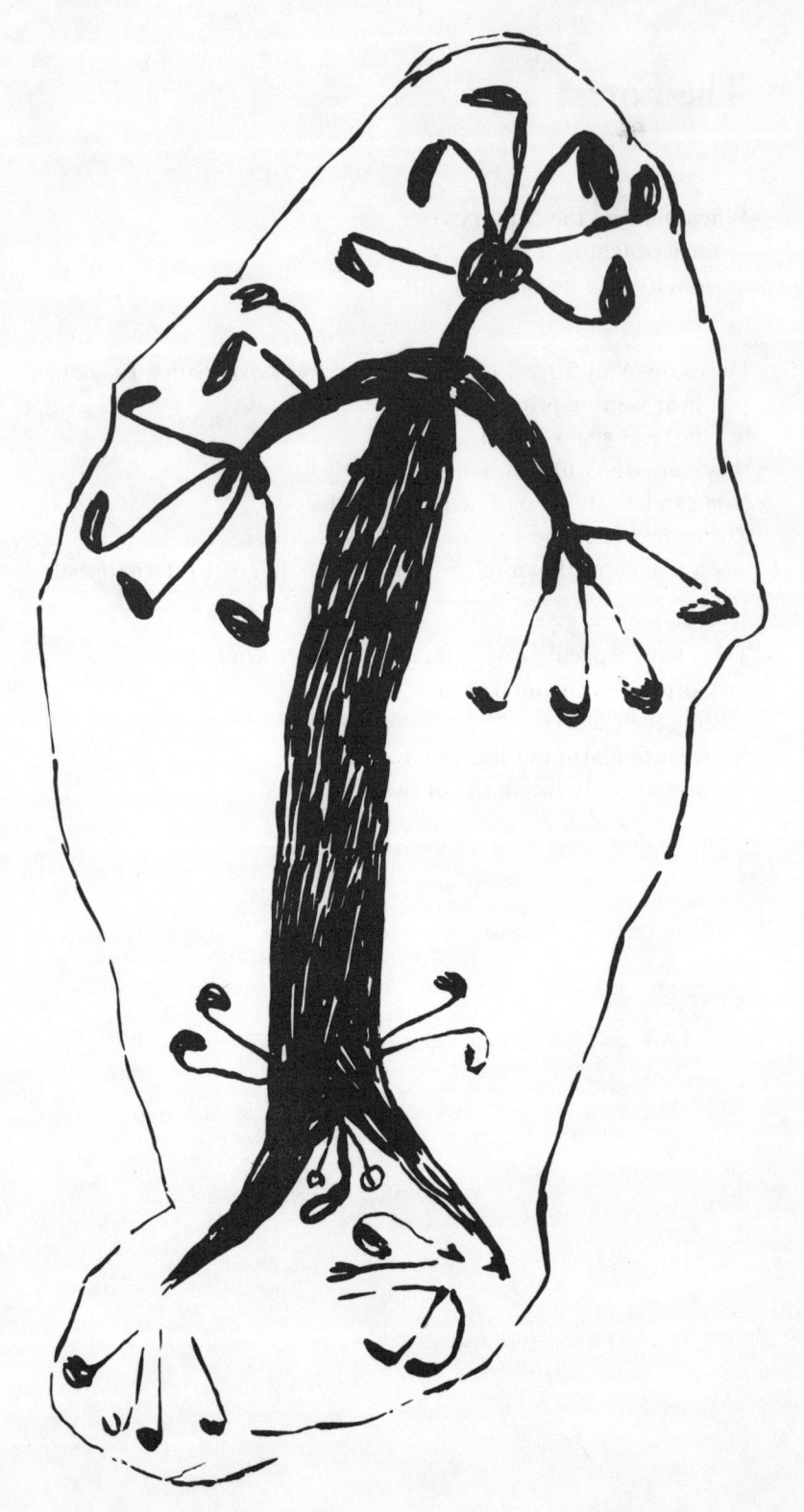

Sugar Glider

> *Among forest tribes, a legend tells of a "waran,"*
> *toddler girl—the lone survivor of a punitive raid*
> *on an aboriginal camp—who changes into a sugar glider*
> *(flying possum), takes off to the trees to live on nectar,*
> *and is seldom seen on the ground again.*

waran . . . waran . . . waran. Fly again
from the top of one tree to another.
Down below, in a chasm of the rain forest,
earth vomits sick with decay.

> In the camp of a trader turned missionary,
> the world has gone from bad to worst;
> red cloth, beads, mirrors, and hatchets
> rebel against a cask of rum. Nearby
> a man resting in a hammock
> draws a picture of Jesus on a slate
> —Dr. Livingstone, I presume.

Glide swiftly between the topmost gums.
When carried on a span of webbed limbs,
life is safe from predators and
drawing slates.

waran . . . *waran* . . . *waran*. Fly from one home of leaves
to another.
In a ravine below, the earth in distress, laments
as a badly wounded beast would groan.
Near the smell of the dead
not even fungus will grow.

Fly.
At the old tribal camp below
the world tiptoes on the blade of a hatchet.

> In no time bullets outnumbered spears.
> Old clubs, fighting sticks, and *ganinjari*
> would all turn into ashes for
> *woomera*, spear-thrower, has died of shame.

Fly over the abyss below.

> Good old Mother Forest trembles
> just as a badly hit snake would do.
> Littered with human limbs, chopped off with machete,
> she laments silently. A broken *galdj*
> hides in the sand. In a white hand
> steel is lethal: dust backed with blood.

Over the abyss.

       In the bush frightened birds lament.
       The trees droop, calling for rain
       to wash away the acrid smell of gunpowder.

waran . . . *waran* . . . *waran*. When tired of gliding
rest inside the fork of a tree.
Among the branches air grows innocent.
Among sun-washed foliage bees make fertility rites
in return for a good crop of nectar. In the abyss below
the world still ferments.

       Fly bravely over leprosy camps,
       camps of typhoid, yellow fever, and high fever,
       over bush infected with steel fever,
       gold fever and everything else
       that has hatched from red cloths,
       beads, mirrors, and Bibles.

Glide and glance down
the abyss, now and then.
Patches of malevolent fungus grow at old camp sites:

       camps of sandy blight of trachoma fame,
       camps of TB, smallpox, and
       far greater pox if you are to tell it all,
       camps of evergreen fungus of VD curse
       spread by the decomposing empire of *balanda*.

Cling to branches, hug the trunk.
During night storms tree hollows whistle
to welcome you to shelter.
In the abyss below

        under the foliage, over blood-saturated soil,
        creeps a new white man's tide
        to spread from an empty bottle
        the smell of decomposing human flesh.

Look out while gliding

        a new malevolent spirit *wardu* hatches from glass.

waran . . . *waran* . . . *waran*. Rise up at dawn
to gather dewdrops from the foliage.
At daybreak all tree shoots grow soft.
Over the abyss, glide over

        poisoned water holes sunk in mud,
        bags of wheat flour blended with arsenic
        —a multitude of horrors; your tongue would cramp
        before it could tell all.

Trees grow much wiser than humans. Fly over

        the plundered country scarred with machetes and hatchets.
        At dead camp below all the cholera bugs
        planted in Red Cross blankets
        have perished after prolonged self-indulgence.
        The forest decimated in the long red-gum purge
        begs for *marngit* and a good rain.

waran . . . *waran* . . . *waran*. Be on the lookout anyhow.
In days of the rusting white man's empire
bush fires happen easily.

Food Gatherer

A handful of ants
gathered on the bottom of *coolamon*
all grown fat on nectar
from *djalg*
from the life-giving tree.

In the red dust, under *djalg*
we all squat.
No one has counted
the ants or the hungry mouths.

In this life of red dust
djalg and the half-empty *coolamon*
objects are not numbered
nor are the rumbling bellies.

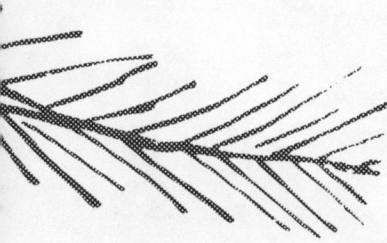

The Tale

They send Itjari, Marsupial Mole,
to spy on Malu, Kangaroo;
for she, his skin sister,
spoke the tribal lingo.

When spying, the animals tiptoe,
same as humans.
When bugging Nagankari, the Medicine Man, though,
one has to crawl;
for Nagankari, like all spirits,
grows long ears.

Malu's telephone was tapped,
                   the mail checked,
                               a file opened on him.
They nick off with his *maban*
—magic shell he makes rain with.
At the time of spooks,
                   pungals,
                              Death Adders.

Nagankari wears wooden legs.

In the waterless country, be aware of *itjari*;
for they, like the Death Adders,
crawl on their bellies.

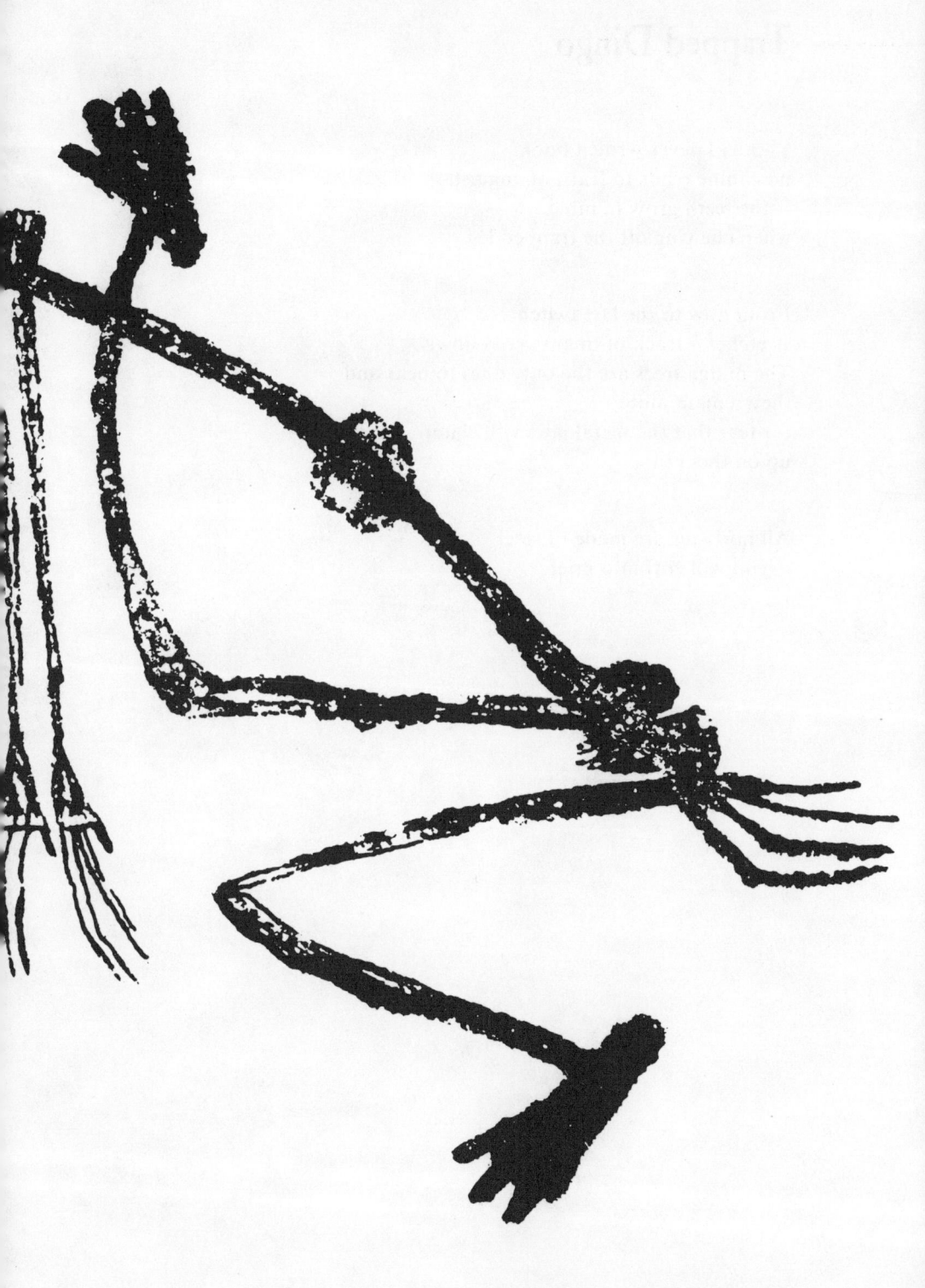

Trapped Dingo

You will never write a book,
no canine reads to learn of anguish
—the teeth grow numb
when chewing off the trapped leg.

From now to the last twitch
stretches a track of unanswered howls.
The mulga trees are the only ones to hear and
they remain mute
for fear that the metal jaws will clamp
up on them too.

All horizons are made of steel
—you will curl into grief.

Jail

You have molded four concrete walls,
set the metal bars,
a lock
to trap the soul.

When inside,
the skin of all *yuln* is equally black;
in the dark
the eyelids stay closed
—the track to Bralgu is known by heart.

Fertility Rites

Bugalili . . . bugalili . . . bugalili!
Jambawal, the Thunder Man,
summons the clouds.
From a wide expanse of water
at *nongaru*, the virgin ground,
black man smeared with red ochre
shapes the boomerang.

Bugalili . . . bugalili . . . bugalili!
Young girls of the inland clans
—blossomed breast held by *maidja*
—sweating young skin smeared with menstrual flow
down at *nongaru*, the virgin place,
pierced by the boomerang.

Bugalili . . . bugalili . . . bugalili!
Over evening sky smeared by menstrual flow
the first clouds are reaching the mainland
to wash maiden blood from *marin*, palm frond,
at *nongaru*, place of Earth Mother.

The Brolgas

A legend tells of a young girl who is seized on her way to "nongaru," the ceremonial ground, to be initiated, and who is taken away to a distant land. She changes into a "brolga" and returns to her native country to dance.

Clat . . . clat . . . clat . . .
In the clattering of your beak
you have gathered
every pair of *bilma* sticks from the country.

Clat . . . clat . . . clat . . .
All the trees in the bush have turned hollow
for wind to play his *didjeridu*.
In the lives of birds, trees, and grass
a *corroboree* has to be held often
to welcome the blossoming of each flower.

Clat . . . clat . . . clat . . .
At salty clay pan near a billabong
ground feathers
float in the air again.

The Journey

To Prue Grieve

You came from a line of felines
with your green thumb, long enough to green the desert,
to land at Wandjina,
caves in the country of *yuln*,
black man.
Those were the days when boomerang refused to bend.

After making the fire from scattered gibbers
you spent the night thinking
of a barefooted black man crossing the Gibson Desert
and praying for drops of rain for a dry water hole.

The felines are grateful to you
so will be *yuln*
if he ever crosses the desert and recovers
from his sore feet.

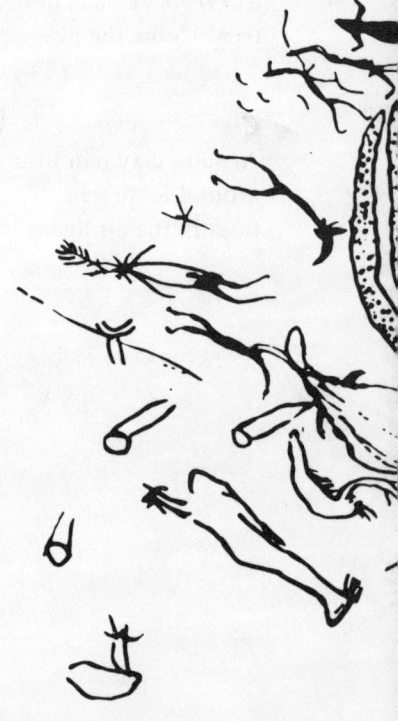

New Gospel

The day God created the world
(according to St. Matthew)
the dark fell earlier than usual.
Crows, crickets, and black man
all turned nocturnal.
So did many other species
the night had long since swallowed.

The Invasion

When the bulldozers crawled out from the sea,
no *yuln*, the tribesman, knew their lingo.
The machines moved in a flock, yelled at by their boss,
to tear the earth. The lot had the pungent smell
of burning tar.
No *yuln* dared to complain
—trees, reptiles, and boulders grew mute.

The bulldozers cleared a clay pan to camp on.
Each gulped a drum of drink, then wallowed in the dust
as *baru*, the crocodiles, do. They rose at dawn;
out to conquer the land,
they puffed and rumbled into dusk.

The machine drained billabongs,
drank all rivers,
dried out the lakes. They took on the mountains
to grind the boulders.

The bulldozers were about to make a sea of sand
when they ran out of puff.
They rust slowly—as the wailing women do
when no *yuln* is left about.

Though the metal rusted
into sand or dust (one can never tell),
yuln, trees, and reptiles never came back
—nor did the boulders.

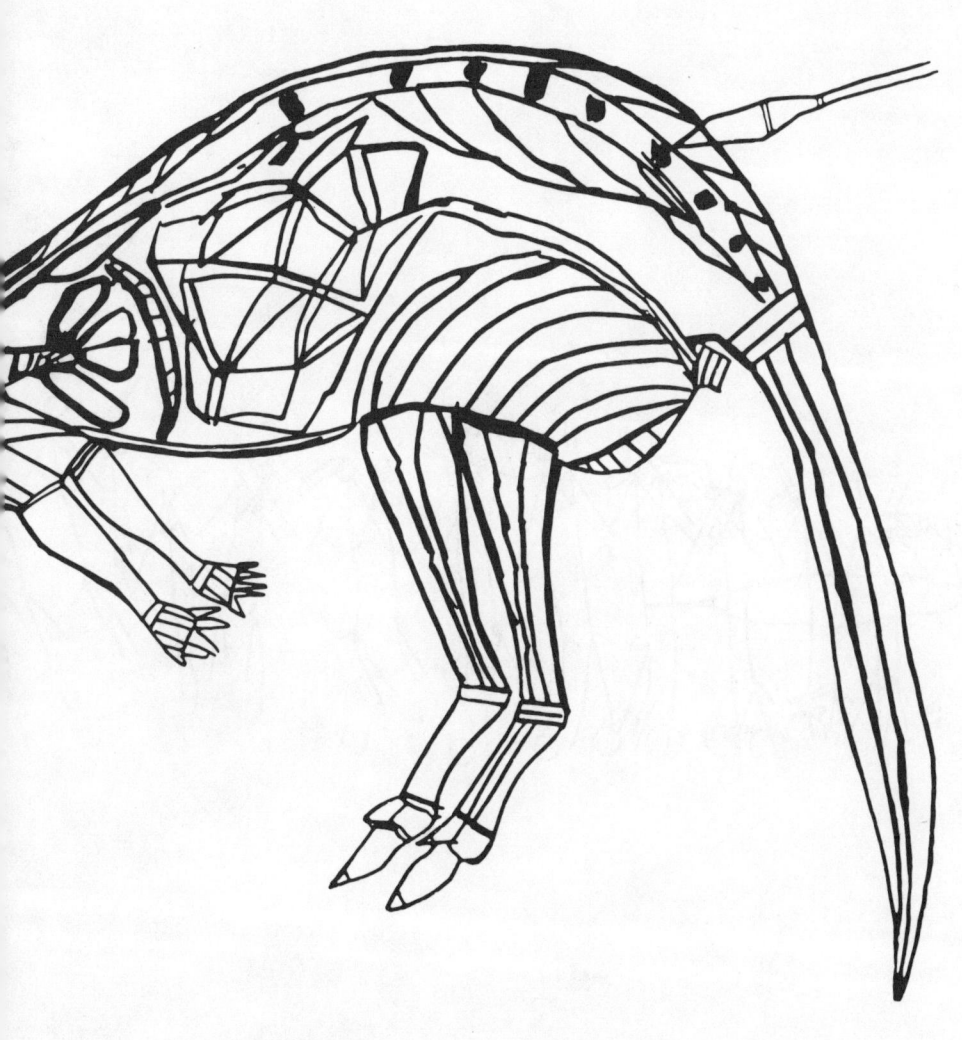

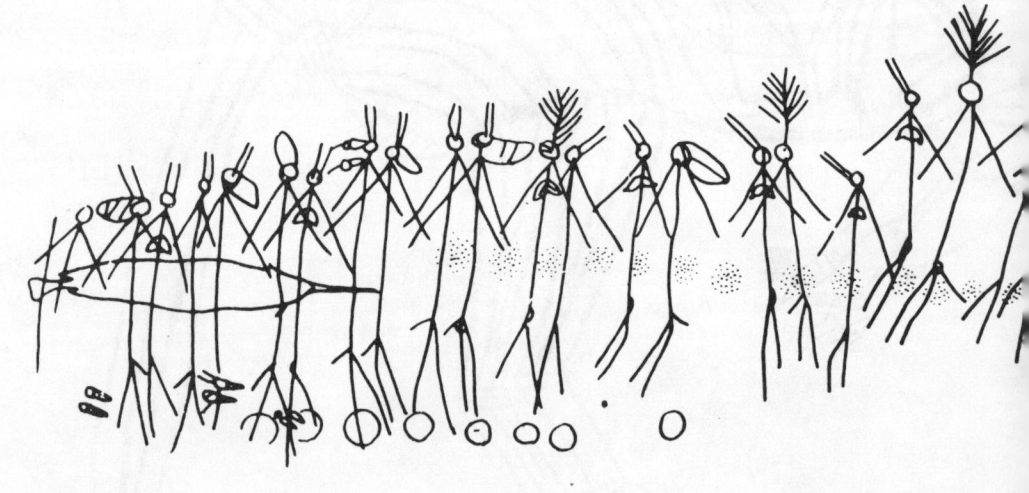

Census

At this day of full moon
every dingo must disclose
his color, height,
                place of domicile.
Print of a front paw
and the assumed date of birth
shall be stamped on his ear.

Warriors of the bush
dare not howl,
                trespass and hunt,
for
the white man commands the guns.

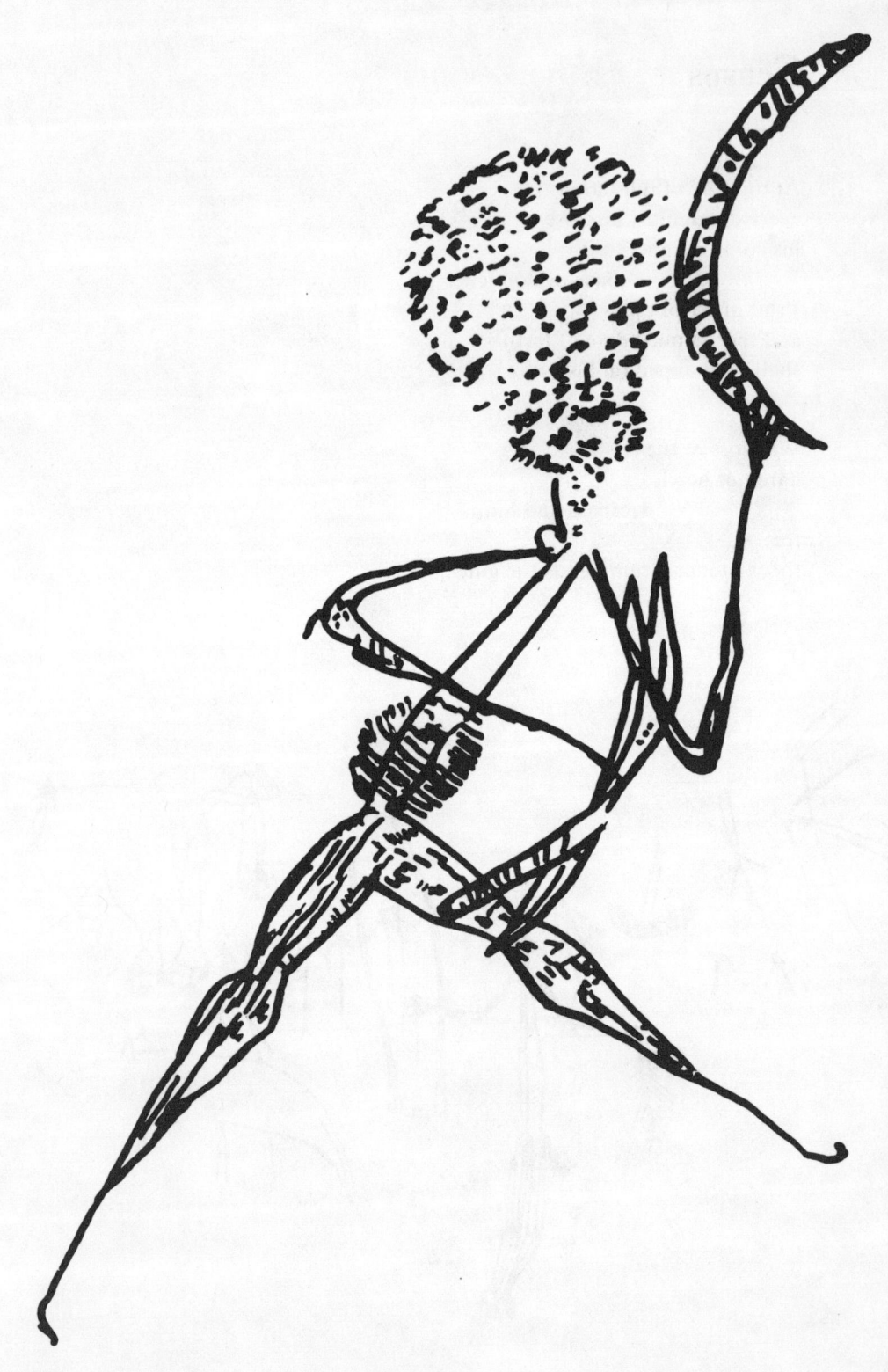

Discovery of the Boomerang

The kangaroo made the first boomerang
not for fun of flying
but to go to the moon
for the moon is a huge damper as
every rumbling belly will tell.
White man came around to nick off the tool
for fun of flying only
as his belly never rumbles. "Give me that device
in name of Progress."

When hidden in pouch
the boomerang could lie flat and still forever.
"Tell us about that flying magic." Kangaroo was chained
in name of God,
               King,
                       Progress.

Kangaroo had no king to swear his allegiance to,
never fought wars and knew of no flag.
"You'll be cut out of the history books," he was told.
Kangaroo did not budge
—history means little if not written by you.
"You'll lose the ration card.
Your water hole is to be polluted.
Your hide shall be fashioned into mink."

When made into a garment
the pouch turns into a pocket, so
the whites find the boomerang.

The Settlers

Messrs. White & Cross had a passion for the hunt.
They used to set out for the bush seeking prey
every Sunday after Mass. No one knew then
that boongs, two-legged game, had furless skin;
for history then was too young to see
and blind like a week-old pup. This happened
when English elms arrived with the First Fleet;
and a century after
Messrs. White & Cross, known locally as squatters,
never had it so good. They refused to die.

When the boongs were all hunted,
Messrs. White & Cross stripped the land; for
the land, too, had the lure of a young tribal maiden.

The name of Messrs. White & Cross is not in the books,
for history, failing to grow up,
behaved as an infant brat
poised to rob every bush nest. After the boongs
the trees departed too.
Messrs. White & Cross ripped open the land
though it had long ceased to be a tribal maiden.
History still refused to come of age;
no one dared belt the badly behaved brat,
for he too went to Sunday Mass
to sing hymns to the English elms.

Pillaged Country

They strip you bone-naked
—when uprooted
trees and rocks turn into wailing mothers
to be silenced only
when a shroud of dust falls over them.

Ah poor fellow my country
we have been together much longer
than the white man can account for.

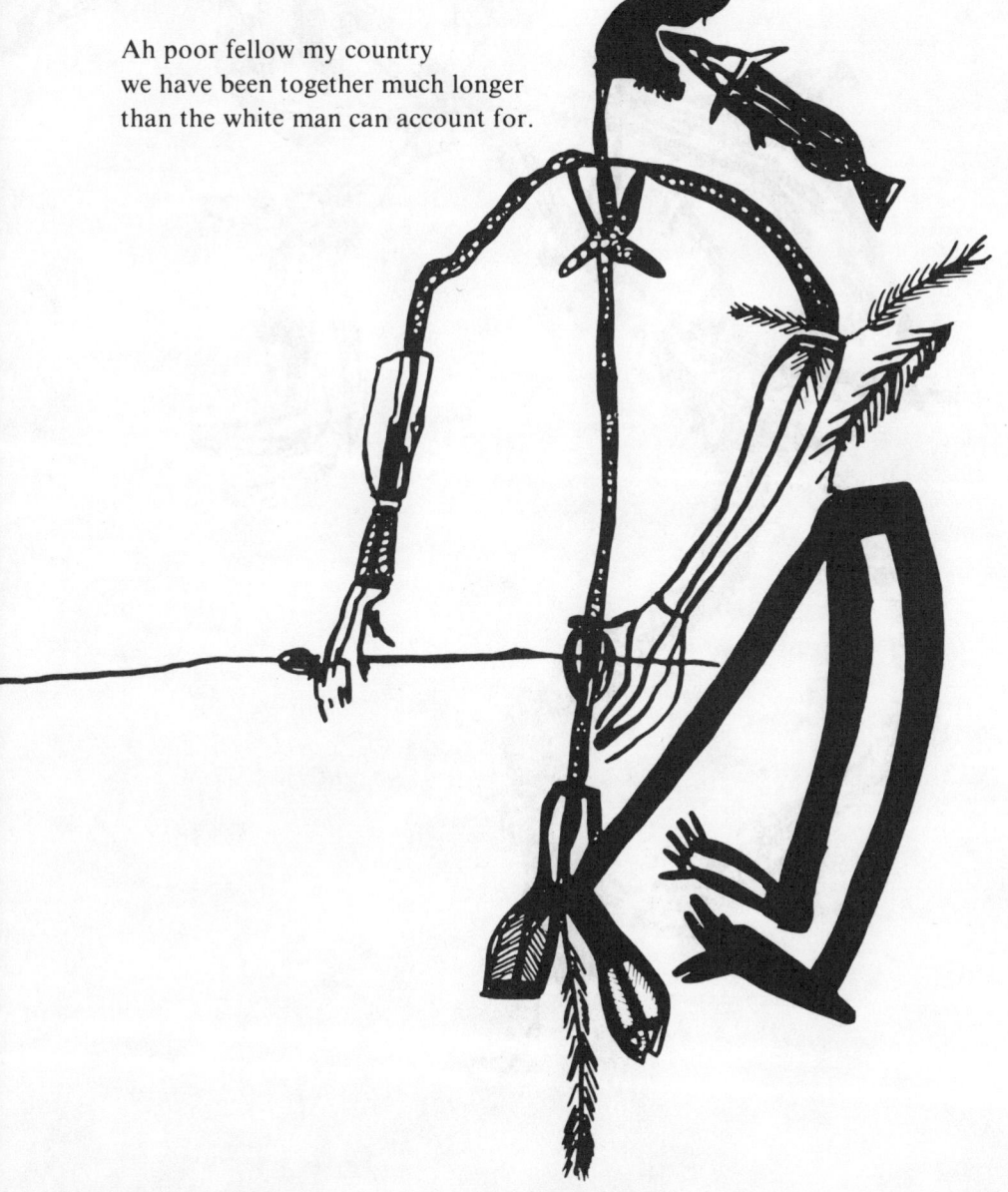

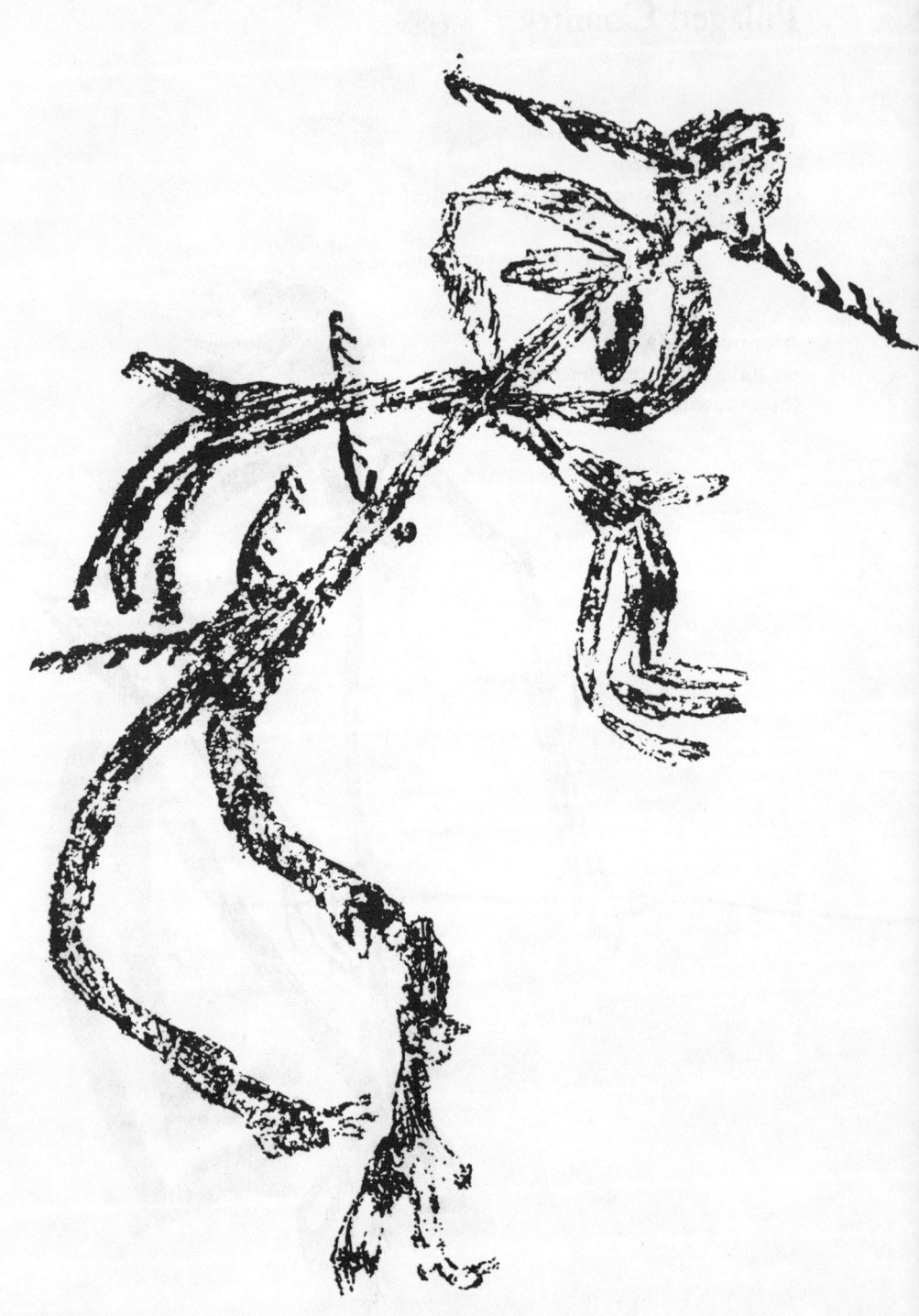

The Conquest

At the time of pirates,
floating monsters, iron, and matches,
Death Adders conquered the world.
With them they brought hatchets, Bibles
—the smell of gunpowder on their index fingers.
The world was too shy then to say much
—no man dares to bark at stars.

Deeath Adders had their King and gods;
they wrote the books and went to Sunday Mass,
just as all cold-blooded reptiles do
before going to seek prey.
Death Adders spread through the bush cutting the trees
as all intruders do when they grow afraid.
A single match spike set the whole country ablaze.
No man lifted his spear and if he had
you would not have heard of him
because history too was written by Death Adders.

Death Adders had their Parliament,
made laws, brief cases and bank accounts.
They played with boulders instead of marbles
christened each rock and trying to make the world flat
ground mountains into dust. Then
Death Adders struck matches to burn the mess
just as every householder does on a decent Sunday afternoon.
By then the good old world must have had enough
—it puffed into flame.

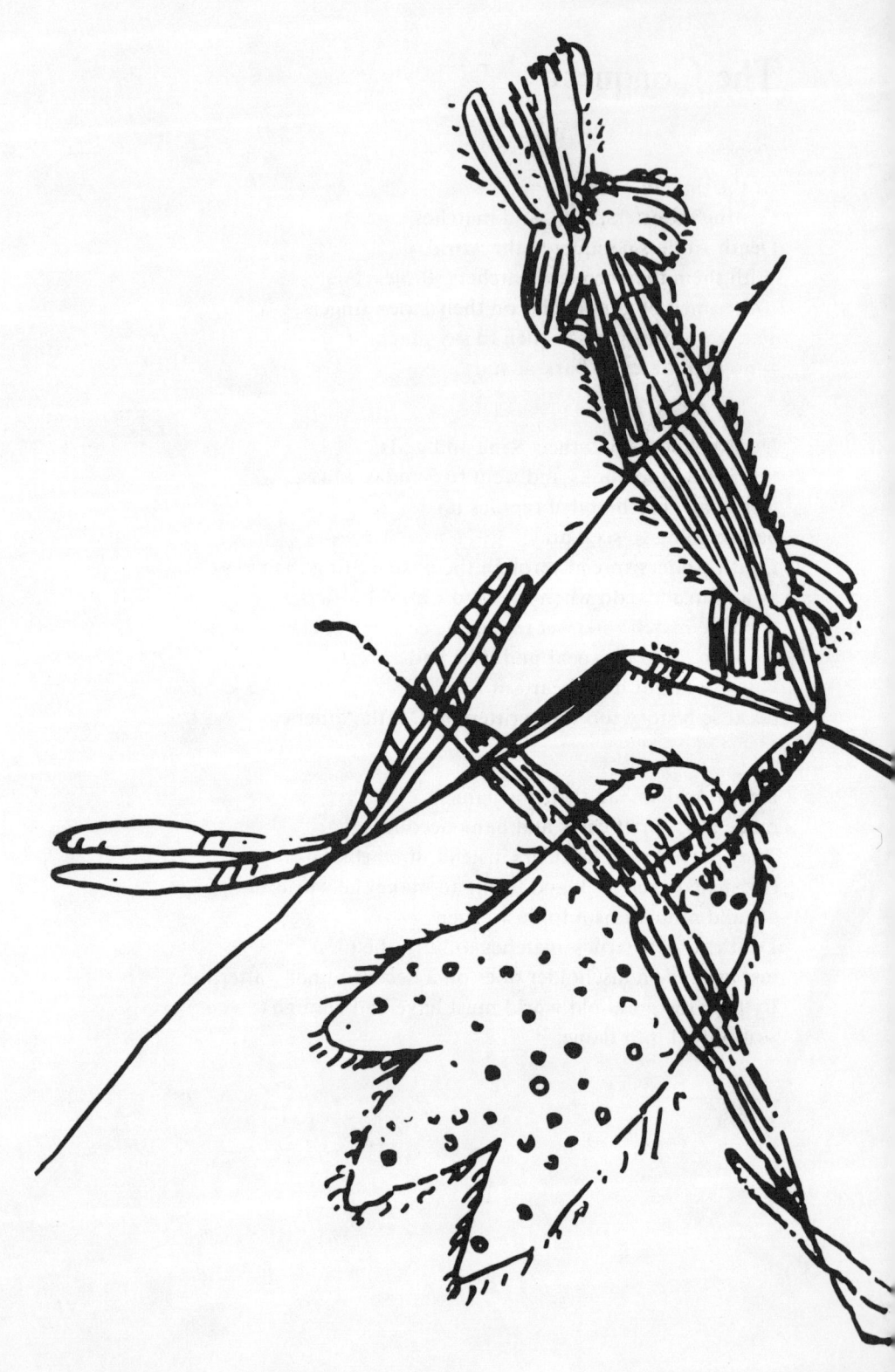

Bilma

Clap . . . clap . . . clap . . .
send the message to Bralgu
—The tide of sand rises fast
to flood the country.

Clap . . . clap . . . clap . . .
the trees grow dry limbs
when buried in sand.

Clap . . .
no *yuln* is left
to clap the sacred sticks
in country swallowed by desert.

Magarada

In the beginning
there were the tribe of trees and the tribe of men.
The two fought savagely just as humans nowadays do
when out from a boring Sunday Mass.

The trees had spears;
the men had *galdj*, stone axes that helped little
against cedars, ashes, and gums.
The trees do breed faster than humans, mind you,
and bleed just the same.

The axes grow blunt.
"Let us have *magarada*, peace treaty," suggested the men.
The trees were told to anchor themselves in the ground forever.
Soon the men threw away the axes. They took hatchets;
saws and bulldozers came later. Matches were brought too
—set ablaze a whole forest.

The trees never broke their word.
"Let us run," suggested the survivors of wood-chip purge.
Though cedars, ashes, and gums
move only a pace or two at a time,
they quickly learn that the world has run out of land.

The Statistics

Mr. Statistic, resident in the capital,
he came here with First Fleet or soon after.
In the beginning Mr. Statistic used to count
rivers, lakes, mountains, and extinct tribes
—no man counted the trees and the spears
for fear of being outnumbered. No explorer ever counted
pebbles in a dry creek bed.
If he had
the humans would soon contract an ulcer
—such was the glory of crossing the continent.

Mr. & Mrs. Statistic live on Van Diemen Avenue.
Is the street any relation to Tasmania?, you might ask.
No, you should not ask;
for their avenue has an English hedge
blossoming often—cherry red.
The avenue is average in length.
Every decent country town has a few Van Diemen Avenues
—which are not to be confused with Van Diemen Gulf,
where all the uranium comes from; for
only boulders, boongs, and their malignant spirits live there,
if they still do.

The Statistics have a cat Tinto (no interest in mining)
and a dog Titan (no relation to ballistic missiles).
The cat was chosen feline of the year.
The canine achieved something too,

though that remains classified. They all live in
Colonel Arthur Masson, as most citizens do
if they are the whites;
for each mansion carries the motto of the founder:
NO ROOM FOR BLACKS.

The Statistics often make a barbecue. When invited,
bring two lamb chops and a can of beer.
You will be told how much ore is quarried per hour,
so many tons of uranium exported per annum. And
when the figures become too complex to state,
they will say as the commoners do,
"So many mountains per year."
They will let you sample the yellow cakes.
Every citizen has to swallow a crumb or two
before tossing the lot to Titan.

When at the Statistics, do not talk about
extinct rivers,
            tribes,
                      and mountains
—the family silver will tarnish
if the guest speaks of the blacks.

Try to smile when munching the yellow cake.
Say no word about poisoned water holes
dried up long ago. The Statistics will not remember
any of it.
Do not talk of the mortality rate
either
—Tinto and Titan have ulcers already.

The Gospel (Contemporary)

According to St. Paul
the black man came late to the world.
Before him there were none around to hold the candle
while the Lord struggled through the night
counting thirteen pieces of silver.

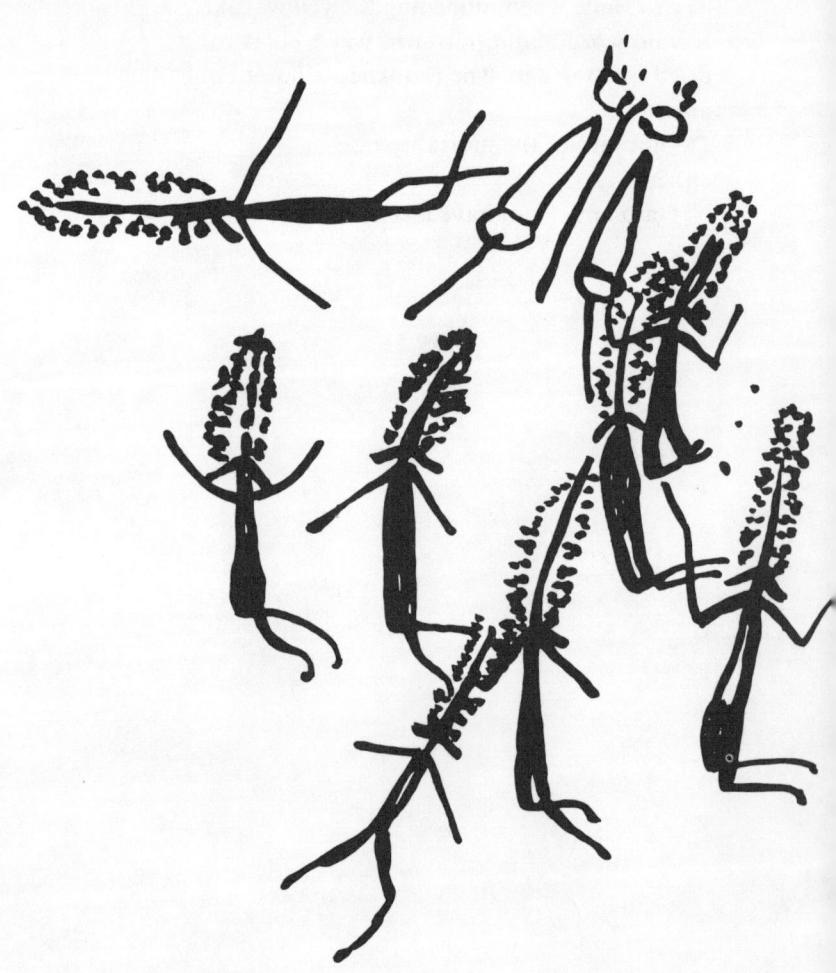

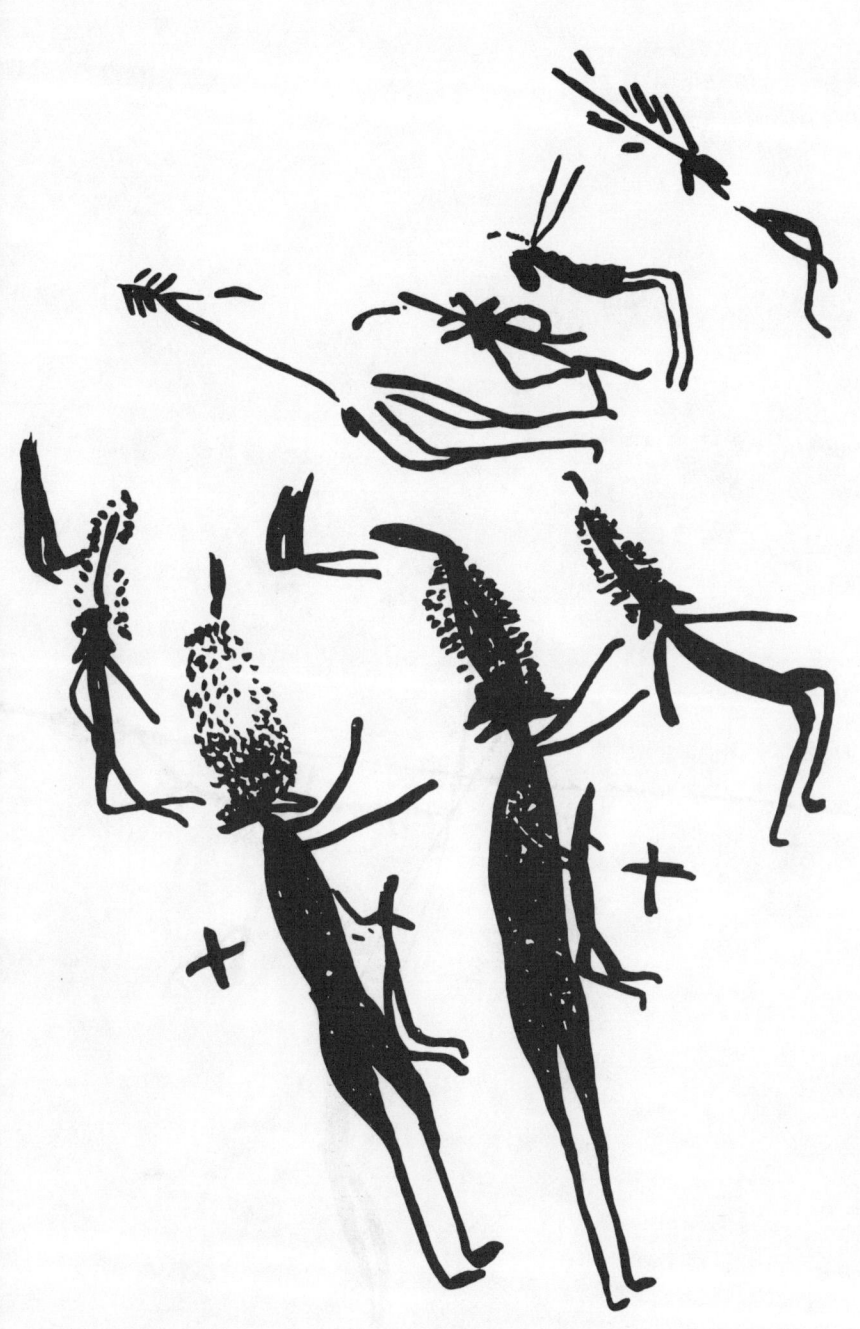

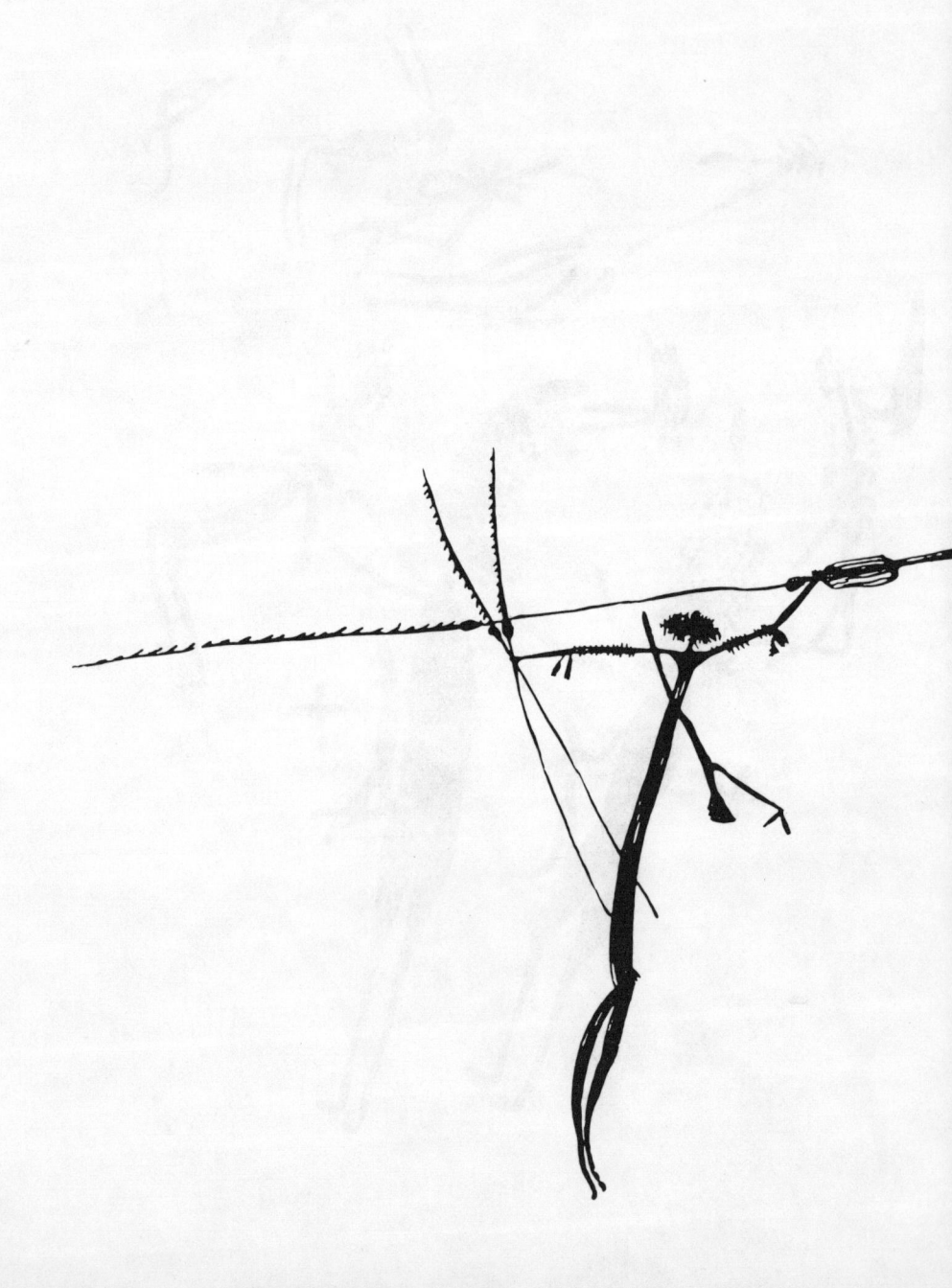

Squatters

The *balandas* made first sheep,
just as anything else they could fleece.
They made paddocks too
—skinned-off patches of land fenced with barbed wire.

The animals breed like white ants
slower or faster
—the *balandas* had to fence whole mainland.
When the land ran out,
they sat down to invent matches
                              axes
                                    and bulldozers
to fleece the country.

Trees, do not tell your skin name, lingo, or *babaru*-clan.
In ashes we are all identical.

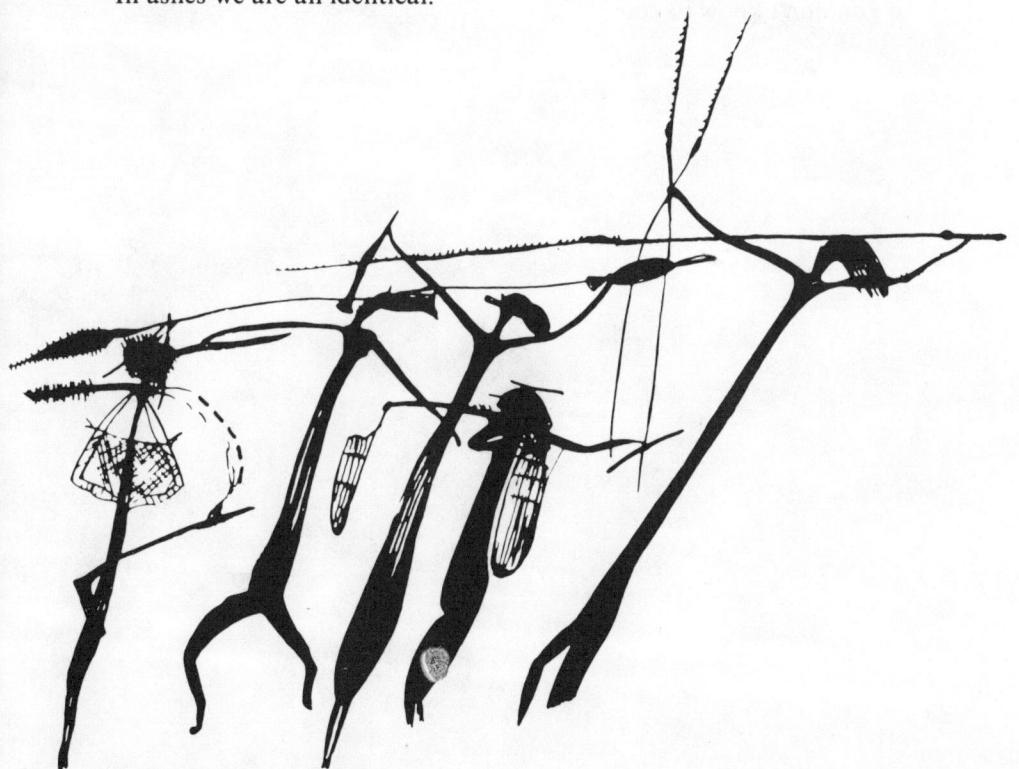

The History

Before the time of the first flowers
giant conifers made large lumps of amber
to give to insects instead of nectar.
The scent of the offerings tasted nice.
Each spring, ferns gathered with mushrooms and moss
for *nara*, the fertility ceremony,
so the lumps grew bigger and bigger.

Much, much later came Elm to rewrite history.
He brought with him a domesticated Willow
to make tea and type the manuscript.
Each tree, grass, and insect had to be renamed,
so did the boulders and rivers.
The plants did not object to a different name,
though most hid away for fear of being cut; but
what is a thousand years of history
if you don't know to count?

"Millions of years," protested Karta, the tree fern.
She refused to budge and yelled to wake up the forest.
"You fruitless bitch
—no book will be written about you," she was told.
She kept wailing, just as *kury*—tribal women—do,
confined in a tub.
"Ill give you a whole chapter to keep quiet," offered Elm.

They christened her *Cyathea australis*.
The words sounded like the lingo of Sunday Mass;
she refused to be urbanized.

In anger, ferns, mosses, and gums
were all cut from history
to make room for Willows and Elms.

Rodingu

On my palm grows a vale
of *wanari*, old mulga trees. Rodingu, my country,
the sand soaked with the sun.

At *pila*, the endless plain,
the spinifex made a last stand
with *intichiuma*, the rainmaking ceremony, then
rode off on the shoulder of the willy-willy,
to the sky.

Rodingu, between me and you,
a wall of mulga trees wails with drooped leaves,
pleading for morning dew. On a sandstone rock,
niari, the lizard our tribe was hatched from,
sharpens his tongue before spears of sun
chase him away.

Between me and you, my Rodingu,
lies the Milky Way paved with bones
of the tribesmen. Rodingu,
so many *kapi*, dry water holes, away.
I will never see you again.

The Cycle

Most pebbles grow into
gibbers,
the gibbers turn into
boulders,
the boulders into mountains.

The mountains would turn
into tribes instead of sand
if *yuln*, the black man,
still had his say.

Jabiru

It could not be precisely determined why or how; but as she descended toward the settlement at Dilaringa, Dilarini realized she had been changed into a jabiru bird. A few hours earlier, she had begun her journey as a human being in a Cessna, and now was going to land as a bird.

There was no need for even the slightest alarm; on the contrary, Dilarini was pleased and scarcely surprised. As a social worker, she had a huge district as her assignment, with the settlements scattered hundreds of miles apart. Now, while airborne, she need no longer worry that the fuel might run out. She felt far more maneuverable; and, being a bird, she could land and take off whenever she wished, irrespective of weather or light.

Dilarini wrote to her boss at the Department of Aboriginal Welfare to inform him of her physical change. She was excited at the prospect of coming closer to the deprived families and over her newly acquired ability to follow them on their traditional walkabout. Being a jabiru, she could camp with the natives under the trees at night and go with them into the scrub during the day to search for lizards and ants to eat. Now, since she was related to the natives of the bird totem, Dilarini expected to gain their confidence and hoped that soon she would achieve a major breakthrough in the search for a solution to the problem of malnutrition and oppression in aboriginal communities.

The boss at D.A.W. did not reply directly, but the Ministry of Welfare announced publicly: "Jabirus will henceforth be withdrawn from the Department's air fleet because of inadequate service facilities. D.A.W. will update its air transport system by introducing Hawks exclusively."

Fertility Ritual

Jambawal, the Thunder Man,
paints the cloud
               white
                       gray
                               black.
At dusk today
a flock of naked *malgu*, flying foxes,
will plunge into the billabong
for a ritual bath. A moon or so after,
the country will grow a green belly,
just as *galei*, the girls, turn
when back from *nongaru*, the initiation ground.

The Dust

When skeletons of dead gums watch moon
an immense desert is around
to wail silently.
In the country of extinct tribes
the spinifex does not remember rain;
humans, birds, and reptiles
have long panted off.

Grains of sand
stay on lookout.
You too might be ground into dust.

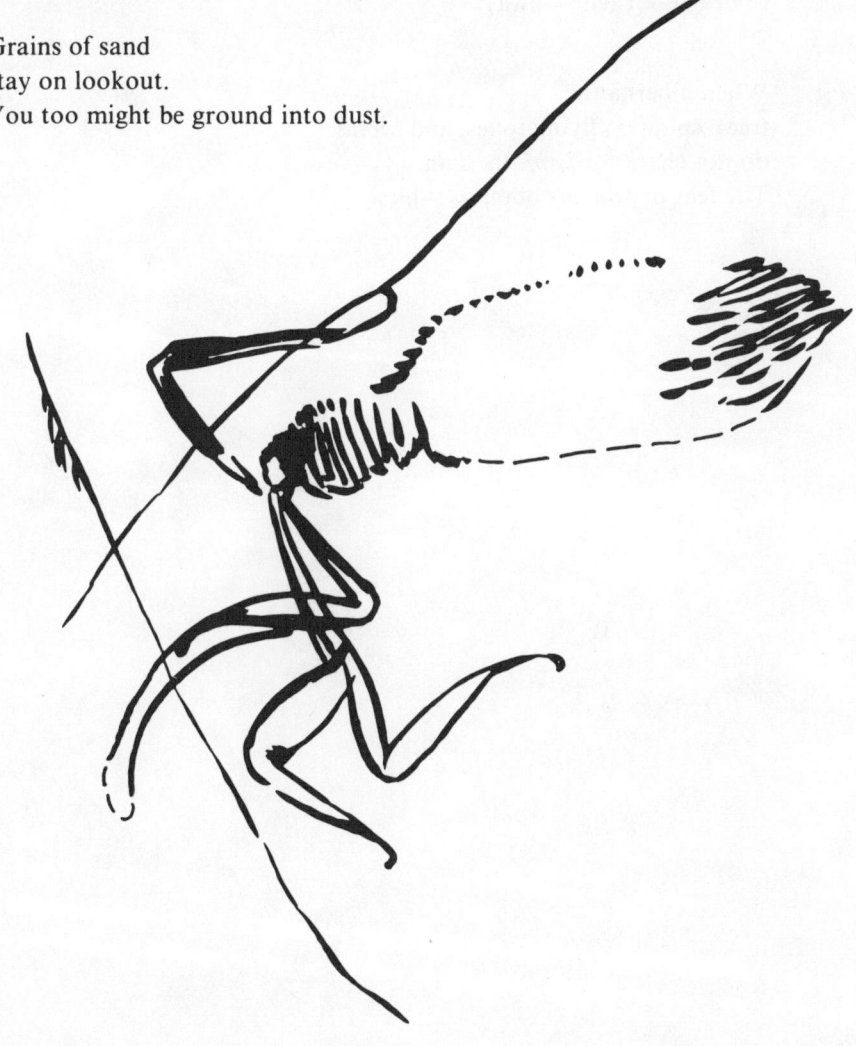

The Drought

When dry, all trees, spinifex,
water holes, and flying foxes
sleep anonymously
as do *tamus*, the tribal spirits.

The day the drought strangled the country
pungals, the whites, noosed a cloud
to drag poor fellow away.

When hibernating,
trees, spinifex, flying foxes, and *tamus*
do not chant for *kapi*, the rain.
The fear of *pungals* outgrows thirst.

U_3O_8

No man held kind words closer to his heart than Bungawa of
Galba Tribe—or so it was said. When the whites reached his
country and began grabbing at the rocks, no angry words were heard
nor curses chanted. The spiritual ancestors who created the
country for tribal man in the Dreaming (but who were now long gone
to Bralgu, land of the dead) must have felt the same way.
None of them came to trouble the minds of the tribal elders, and
it looked as though, wherever the whites were keen to dig and
to grind the rocks, no harm would come to the black man and
his spirits.

Bungawa found it hard to grasp why anyone would bother with
rocks. The boulders had no taste and only patches of lichen grew
on them. A paper brought to him to sign hardly told him
anything; it referred to rocks and U_3O_8—a formula he had never
heard of before and that undoubtedly had no tribal importance.
The U was too bent to symbolize a boomerang; and the O, though it
was the shape of the egg of the totemic serpent, appeared too
small to have any spiritual significance. And as for the numbers,
Bungawa could find nothing like them in the tribal world.
He placed his thumb on the place marked "Signature" at the bottom
of the paper. "The whites have strange rituals," he told the
people later. He appealed to every tribal soul to respect the
arrangement, however strange it sounded.

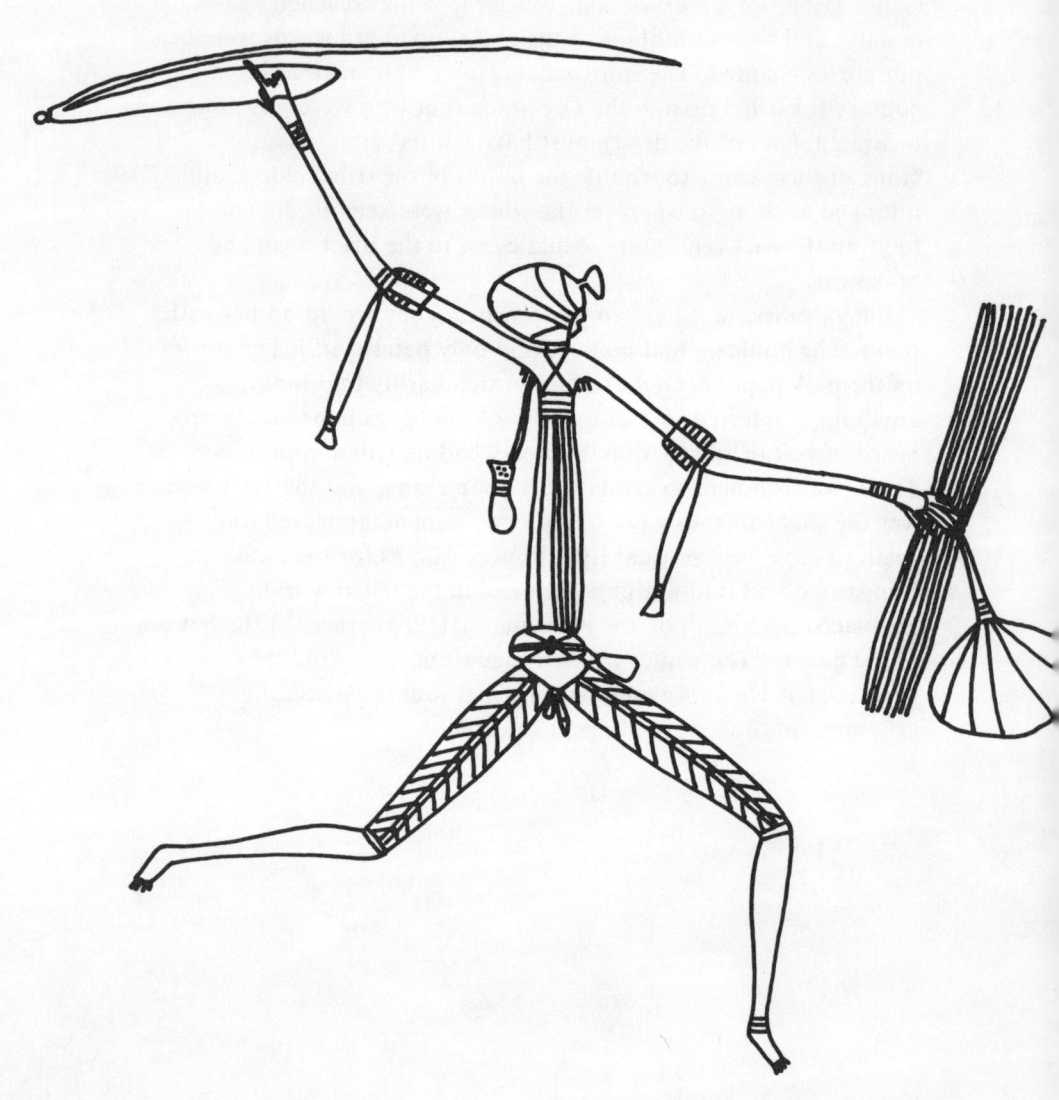

Much later, Bungawa learned that U_3O_8 is commonly called "yellow cake." If it had not been for his standing as a wise old man, the news would have set him laughing. Instead he wondered how the rocks would taste when ground into dust and baked to make a yellow cake. He was wise enough to know that, though personal tastes differ as much as colors of the human skin, a man eats only what his stomach can manage.

Tasteless and tough as the rocks were, they were not given away for nothing. When the whites came to take them, they brought bags of tea and boxes of biscuits; and each tribal elder received a packet of tobacco and a steel axe. Bungawa, presented with a stainless steel pipe and a bottle of rum, felt that, however odd the tastes of the whites might seem, trading with them could be pleasant. The mountains at Galba were large enough to last for years; but should the country run out of boulders, Bungawa would gather the elders, clap two wooden sticks together, blow the *didjeridu*, and chant for the ancestors to come and make new hills again. At the end, when the whites no longer needed the yellow cake, the chanting would be needed again to bring back the trees and the scrub to the barren earth. The scars on the land would heal quickly.

Bungawa went on a trip around the world carrying a dilly bag
full of rocks, hoping to whet the white man's appetite. The
tribal country he left behind lay under a cloud of dust too
leaden for even the monsoon wind to carry away. Little was heard
and less seen of Galba for years; but it was always thought
that, however thick the hanging dust cloud might be, it would
eventually fall back onto the tribal ground and the ancestors
would be there to see that the bush grew up again.

Even though hopes remained sky high, the tribal country never
greened again. From the settling dust rose hills of mining waste,
bare and dry. Bungawa wandered among them, blowing his *didjeridu*
now and then to gather the tribal elders to join him with their
clapping sticks and chanting. But no one came. With the going of
the bush, man had departed too. The new shape of the country
was no place even for a fly.

Instead of the spirit world of Bralgu, the blowing of the
didjeridu reached the white man's world. Bungawa received a flood
of telegrams wishing his country a speedy recovery. The bells
of Canterbury Cathedral rang for a whole week. Ayatollas sent
their prayers, and Stravinski was commissioned to dedicate a
concerto to the tribal cause.

The effort achieved nothing. Little patches of lichen grew
here and there on the crushed boulders, but the leaves never came
again. The country remained dry and dead; and Bungawa knew that if
even an ant happened to appear there, it would be drowned in
a sea of dust.

Bralgu

Nganug the paddle-maker
ferries the dead
far across the sea
to land of *yuln*.

The canoe will be around
on time to fetch the last man
of the last tribe.

When Nganug dies
who will ferry him?

An Epitaph

In the country of merino ram,
beefsteaks, and
stockpiles of U_3O_8,
extinct tribes are not accountable for.

Neither are *buwad*, the flies.

Glossary

babaru—a family
balanda—a white man
baru—a crocodile
billabong—a pool of backwater
bilma—clapping sticks
boong—a derogatory term for aborigines
Bralgu—Land of the Dead
brolga—a bird (*Crus rubicunda*) of gracious behavior, about the size of a turkey
bugalili—a ritual invocation meaning "Revive. Come to life again."
buwad—a fly
clay pan—a flat area of hardened clay
coolamon—a wooden dish or bowl
corroboree—a ceremony or dance ritual
damper—an unleavened loaf baked in the ashes of a campfire
didjeridu—a wind instrument made from a hollow tree that produces deep notes
djalg—a paperbark tree
Dreaming, the—Myth of Creation
galdj—a stone axe
galei—a girl
ganinjari—a digging stick
gibbers—oval stones covering some Australian deserts
intichiuma—ceremonies, life-increasing rites
itjari—a marsupial mole
Jambawal—Thunder Man
kapi—a water hole, rain
karta—a fern tree
kury—a woman, women
maban—a sacred seashell used in rainmaking rituals
magarada—a peacemaking ceremony

maidja—a breast girdle worn by girls
malgu—a flying fox or bat
malu—a kangaroo
marin—a cabbage palm
marngit—a healer or medicine man
nagankari—a term used in central Australia to denote a medicine man
namanama—native country
nara—a fertility ceremony
Nganug—Paddle Maker, Ferryman
ngir—a cicada
niari—a thorny lizard (*Moloch horridus*)
nongaru—a ceremonial ground used for the initiation of girls into adulthood
pila—a semidesert plain
pungals—a term used in central Australia to denote both malovent spirits and the white man
Rodingu—a place of totemic significance in central Australia
sandy blight—a common name for trachoma
spinifex—porcupine grass (*Triodia irrutans*)
sugar glider—a flying possum
tamus—spirits, tribal ancestors
wanari—the mulga tree
Wandjina—caves in northern Australia sacred to the Aborigine
waran—a flying possum
wardu—a term used in northern Australia to denote malevolent spirts
willy-willy—a dust storm
woomera—a spear thrower
yellow cake—a common or slang term for uranium oxide
yuln—tribal man or aborigine